C000085048

JALUBÍ

Emily Paige Wilson

JALUBÍ

Copyright © 2022 EMILY PAIGE WILSON

All Rights Reserved.

Published by Unsolicited Press.

Printed in the United States of America.

First Edition.

No part of this book may be used or reproduced in any manner
whatsoever without written permission except in the case of brief
quotations embodied in critical articles or reviews.

Attention schools and businesses: for discounted copies on large orders,
please contact the publisher directly.

For information contact:

Unsolicited Press

Portland, Oregon

www.unsolicitedpress.com

orders@unsolicitedpress.com

619-354-8005

Cover Design: Kathryn Gerhardt

Cover image provided by Emily Paige Wilson

Editor: Gage Greenspan

ISBN: 978-1-956692-15-0

for my family: Bobby, Kathryn, Ryan, Trent, and Meredith

in memoriam: Jason Bradford and Jacqueline Winter Thomas

I never dream of speech:
I either speak or don't.

——

Of what is this
gesture
the ancestor?

—Christina Davis

Contents

JALUBÍ

Rovně a Doprava

Beneath a row of witches, she sweeps
the sidewalk in front of her souvenir shop.
                          I've wandered past
my map's reach.

                         We are alone
         with the cobblestones and cold
light of streetlamps sweating
copper shadows on our faces.
                       Her back bent
more fantastic than the gnarled handle
in her grasp. Each evening breeze
breathes flight

into the pulpit of puppets above.
                            I am not afraid
of women made mythical and immoral,
                 spinsters with snarled spines.

I fear instead the loud thoughts
that taunt the lost, those who cannot find home
without being shown where to go.

Promiňte, I ask

permission to break the silence
the street has laced

       like a shawl around her shoulders.
Kde je metrem?

She answers in a spell of syllables indiscernible to my ears.

Finally she casts a glance far into the dark.
        Rovně a doprava.
  Doprava, I repeat, my tongue an apprentice
in unfamiliar sounds.
      Díky, I offer.
Hezký večer into the hazy navy
of the night.
    Doprava. Straight

       and to the right.

I. Departure

Reasons to Learn Another Language

—after Cecilia Llompart

Because verbs only move if tongues
do. Because there is a no man's land

where all of the mouth's mistakes are
allowed: teethlings tripping sounds

to tatters. Because *untranslatable* is just
a challenge. Because your jaw gets bored.

Because *You are missing from me* means
much more than *I miss you*. Because

everyone wants to tell you their name
in the way that feels most familiar. Because

not all facial expressions are universal,
not even the ones for pain. Because

some people are forced to give up
their alphabet in order to assimilate.

Because consonants can often not.
Because you and a stranger can stare

at the same water, but if you don't share
a word for *please*, then you are both still

thirsty. Because lineage is a lace that frays.
Because my stutter—a string of sounds arrested—

is still an attempt. Because we wouldn't
be able to tell the sky from the sea

had the color blue decided not to divide itself.

Conjugation

A bringing   across: to bear, to burden. We are

only land   locked in the strictest sense, with

strict   being a measure in mountain mass. To

burn.   Thieves, in tiredness,

in thirst,   have stolen

                                  vowels

from *death*, from *frozen solid*.   They will be returned

only once   we accept the pluperfect.

What false   stepping stones these consonants

offer.   A source language

laden coarse with silt,   with a slitting of the tongue:

to turn, to tarnish.   What has happened once

can continue to happen: to hunt, to haunt.

The density of our decibel   will not float.

A language with three tenses is a body   without sinew,

silence,   or snare.

Baking Lessons

Across the kitchen counter, my grandmother kneads
koláče dough. The walls are goldenrod, puckered
as the pastries. Warmth has made a womb of this room,

of the thumb-pressed pockets
she fills with poppy seeds.

Grandma, I ask,
what's love like?

She says, *The love of a sister is a deep
stain, the way plums purple everything.*

No, grandma. Not like that.

She says, *A mother's love is a dumpling,
how its body plumps to meet your cheeks.*

No, gramma, no.

She says, *A daughter's love is sour
cream, cool yet prone to curdle.*

She places small suns in each palm,
peach jam glazes lazily in their pits.
Cheese and cherries, chipped platters
on which the sweets are stacked.

No, grandma! Love! What is real love like?

Oh, that! Well, real love, she says,
is the sound a fork makes
   as it scrapes
   a plate
     clean.

Photograph: My Great-Grandmother Gladys as Bride

St. Ludmilla Catholic Church
Chicago, 1940

Scalloped and yellowing, the frame itself is buttercream.
Everything   in the image spills
over. A ring of the groom's   dark hair on his forehead;
the bride's lace veil as it lifts   and lowers; the laughter
a bridesmaid tries   catching in a cupped hand.
The bride   is all cheeks and crinoline;
groom   with a mischievous
windswept
grin.

I can see

my mother's face   in the bride's
the way I see   my own
reflected in a pool of water: luminous and distorted.

The Fortune Teller Predicts a Journey

Patchouli's mossy morning breath
edges out of incense. The teller spreads

purple velvet across the table between us,
teases tea lights into flame with the crass

scent of a handful of matches. I am all
cups and swords, more Major Arcana

than she usually sees drawn by a single hand.
I was first taught to seek the Tarot as a child.

On my grandmother's night stand, her deck sat
near stacks of photo albums. She'd compare

The Wheel of Fortune's zodiac disc to Prague's
astronomical clock, how similar their concentric

golden circles. Or, mane ablaze, the lion
of *Strength* and the beast of Bohemia stamped

on the back of all Czech coins. We'd sift
through the cards before shifting to the

photos, lives lifted and cropped into gray-
scale squares. Nine children aligned

in ceremonial dress; girls in polka skirts,
boys held up in suspenders. Their stern

matriarch, dark hair twisted into a sloppy
top knot like the jewel-encrusted headdress

of *The Empress*. Even with these faces, grandma
could only remember fractions — certain branches

of the family tree. Had only been given
a rough phonetic spelling of the village

her grandparents once left: *Jalobee*. I've learned
to read the deck the same way I read my family

history: to leave space for the stories
once names and dates have faded.

When the fortune teller reveals *The Hermit*,
lone figure cloaked against the cold, she

cannot read his direction. I have learned
to love stories with visible stitches,

to be content with only best guesses.

The Old Country

CZECHOSLOVAKIA 1887 painted
on the porcelain base of Saint Nicholas.
White wizard beard, sack slack across his shoulder.

Every Christmas, the chipped china ornaments
are unpacked, arranged in the clink and rustle
of tinsel and tissue. My sister strings lights;

my brothers dollop dough onto baking sheets.
We are most Czech this time of year:
dumplings doused in plum sauce, blood

sausage and sauerkraut. We call it *the old
country*, but what we mean is *not here,
too far removed*. A country we have never been to

cannot age, remains unchanged in our minds.
My sister bores quickly of unboxing
glass bulbs. She peeks on my mom,

trapped in a mass of wrapping
paper, then walks to the window
and waits for snow that won't fall

this warm Carolina winter. A plastic
evergreen branch bends with the weight
of Saint Nicholas. MADE IN CHINA

stamped on its side. There are
many ways to speak of this loss—

> This is all the Czech left
> to us. This is all the Czech left
> for us. This is all the Czech left
>
> of us.

I Dream of Trains Before Leaving

On a train named *Turbidity*, two passengers are tousled
out of memory. Who among them the thief,
who the translator? A haunting inhabits
this heat, this hearth into which
coal is shoveled and steam emerges
worried and wild as a whistle.
What if the destination is
merely submergence? The surface
shaken into a kaleidoscope,
stirring sediment to refract river
water. To taste the saltiness
of a noun before knowing
its declension. Spectrums spasm
off the approaching water. The translator
whispers to the window, "*Coincidence* from
the Latin *to sink*." His reflection answers back:
"But think of what our stolen suffixes can change."

Retrospect

We buried a national archive
after my great-grandmother died.
What was left of her life
now stored in torn journals.
The details of her dancehall husband,
an immigrant she taught English,
the daughter of Czechs herself.
Vocabulary vetted between swing steps.
Her visits to people she didn't even know
who had been left alone in cancer wards
because doctors still warned against contagion.
Time spent editing small town papers
when women weren't allowed to work for the press.
Asking her granddaughters to roll dumpling dough
once arthritis curved her knuckles in its control.
My last memory of Gladys is from before I left for Prague.
She said, "We worked so hard to raise you right,"
and then—"Make us proud; find a good Czech man to marry."

———

Gladys said, "Find a good Czech man to marry,"
and then—"We worked so hard to raise you right."

This is my last memory of her before I left for Prague.
Her knuckles in the curled control of arthritis.
She'd ask us to roll out dough for dumplings.
Before, when most women weren't allowed to work,
those hands ran red edits in small town papers.
Before, when doctors warned against contagion
and patients were left alone in cancer wards,
she'd visit people she didn't even know.
Between swing steps, she vetted vocabulary—
a daughter of Czechs herself—
teaching English to an immigrant
at a teenage dancehall, her future husband.
Now it's all stored in torn journals:
what's left of her life.
After my great-grandmother died,
we buried a national archive.

My Great-Aunt Speaks of Gladys

—original text provided by Victoria Vlach Hughes

"Gladys and Frank made a good couple because they not only loved each other, they challenged each other. They often disagreed; they also often danced. They met at a dance hall. When she met Frank, he wanted her number so he could call her to meet again. She didn't give it to him but said she would be back there the next weekend. She wanted to see if he would be there to see her. She and her sister went back the next weekend and Frank was there all by himself waiting for her at the door. As they say, the rest is history."

———

           they   loved   they challenged

They   disagreed they s often   ed.   at a dance all

he wanted

                was   her

———

                they   loved

     t   o   dance

Passport

A country of origin in a grandmother's jewelry box. Old and ornate, baubles heavy on the lobe. Garnets are the stone of the city, the stone of my birth. The city is built in spires. My ears are not pierced.

Orientation: *Promiňte, kde je metrem?* Straight, then to the right. *A kde jsou moji duchové?* Saving you a seat on the train.

Legacy: Blood is fractal as opposed to fractional. Bronzed branches on autumnal oaks are not ¼ alchemists.

Translation: If you are in Old Town, you are in Old Town. If you walk across a bridge, you are in Malá Strana. What is the latitude of your language now?

Threshold: (See also: pain.) The point at which this vision begins to take on properties of the nightmare. He broke his sandal on the doorframe. Look for the detached leather strap round his foot as he toils in the field and call him king. Libuše loosened into myth. You do not yet know you do not come from here.

Pronunciation: A háček is the difference between halve and have.

II. Arrival

Learning to Speak Czech: A Homophonic Translation

Nemluvím česky.
Navigate carefully.
Newly muffled clicking teeth.
Nevermind speaking.

Nerozumím.
Neat rows of symbols newly minted. Neat rows of symbols
newly minted. Net zero meaning.
I do not remember.

Jak se jmenujete?
The first time I heard a woman
besides my mother
say my name, I was lost
in the shock: how sound
is not a belonging
bound only to one mouth.

Jak se řekne česky "_____"?

You see red-kneed children,
dancing, their readied chests
aching for the right key.

Say reckless.
Say restless,
wrecked. Say weight.
Waiting in my cheeks "all this empty space"?

Reasons to Travel to Another Country

Because you do not know if you are
the coordinates or the compass.

Because borders blur like the burn between
red and orange. Because there is courage

in courting words you cannot say correctly, but
still trying anyway. Because your palm fragmented

into a five-fingered path is your body's warning
about staying in one place for too long.

Because the ocean holds a familiar song,
but only if you don't forget where you heard it

first. Because my family has a picture of a farm
and not much else. Because who will remind you

how fragile your face is? Because only those
who have seen the aurora borealis still believe

they are holy. Because not all origin stories
were sworn to tell the truth. Because some

things that haunt you are bound to the land
you live in. Because you are the coordinates

and the compass. Because each mountain range
is the earth's birthmark, and you would not leave

your lover's body so unturned.

Introductions

Petr and Stana have agreed to be my parents
for the four months I'll study in Prague.

As I unpack in their flat, Stana
promises to take me to her garden; Petr

to the pond where he taught his children
how to skate. Both Eliška and Vitek,

thirteen and eight, speak English with ease.
I can't remember how to say *thank you*

in Czech, so I mumble *prosím* profusely,
a polite word I'm afraid will split at the seams

each time I speak. I think about how much
of our personality is woven into the words

we say, how gracious can quickly be mistaken
for uncomfortable if sounds are scattered

too far. I think *language barrier*, though nothing
blocks our bodies but empty space.

Stana leads me to a bedroom with freshly
plumped pillows and sweet-smelling sheets.

I think *mother tongue*, yet nothing
is maternal about stalled speech.

Speech is more of a child. We raise
it through mistakes, swaddle the sounds

in our mouths, rock them in unsteady rhythm.

I Forget the Czech for "Stamp" in the Post Office and Start Making Up Words Instead

the number of times you must
say   any   name   out   loud
to make a spell of the sounds: reporacle

> msytory: a measure of how much any myth
> borrows   from   truth

the promise the bridge sells
you in return for massaging
its arched and aching back: susstrict

> circumtheft: stealing something only to find
> you   can't   use   it;   see   also:
> the space the rain takes as it falls

Karlův Most

I could tell you were in need
when I noticed how you lay
your most revealing mirrors

underneath. Only the hungry
insist on reflecting the least
flattering facet of the self.

Straight stretch of sandstone
heavy and earnest as my tongue
pronouncing *Vltava* for the first time.

Did you know, depending on
declension and angle of incidence,
your name becomes my home

state in English? English: that linguistic
Atlantic into which all sounds are forced
to channel. We translate most rivers

in our cowardice. I will take
pictures of you, dear bridge,
at a diagonal. Half your saints

will feel safe, half will always
taste the fear of sinking.

Transaction

—*after Yiannis Ritsos*

It is cold in the market. A woman who knows no
Czech can't tell how much to pay the peddler
for his bread. She pushes gold circles
across her palm and pretends to
count. Her finger shivers and
slips. A few coins fall to the
ground, a string of heated
clinks, like autumn's
spine snapped in
half by winter's
weathered
teeth.

After sounds, words.
After the words, sounds again.

Skating

We drive two miles to a postcard
pond. Gray glint perimeter, slate
landscape broken only by a few blades

of yellowed grass too stubborn to grasp
they will not grow in the cold.

Vitek glides away as soon as we reach
the ice, but Petr stays and steadies me

while I lace my skates. Petr is patient.
He clasps my elbow, explains how to shift
my weight hip to hip while pressing forward

into the bitter whistle of February's breath.
With each push and plunge, I crumple
in the knees. Petr's by my side until
I can guide my blades into well-worn

figure eights. He leaves only to let me
balance on my own. His voice has
the same tenderness as my dad's
when he taught me how to play pool,

or to not grow angry when I couldn't
figure out the right angles for a shot.
My thoughts wander so far that when

I remember where I am, I lose
balance and collapse. My nerves

scatter in a storm of pulse and pinch,
back flat to ice, black behind my lids.

Petr and Vitek skate over, pull me
up. "It is not so bad," Petr says.

    "Your first time falling
    could've been much worse."

Quilling

Every morning, Stana stirs a sunset
on the stove: pumpkin soup for dinner,

ginger and carrots grown in her garden. She
brews ruby rose hip tea when she hears me
sniffle in my sleep, spends evenings

teaching her children English, listening to
their late-night violin lessons. When they go
to bed, Stana can finally quill. She shows me

this art: rolling, shaping, pasting paper
into flowers and other designs. Thin strips
into teardrops, loose coils, and spirals.

Tight blue corkscrews for baby toes
she pastes on a card for a pregnant friend.
I watch her in the dark hours and think

of my mother's crocheting: blankets and scarves
in the winter for every third-grader in her class.
Chain stitch, slip stitch. The slippery sounds

and little wrist flicks of these women
and their work: all tiny lessons in patience.

Pražský Orloj

Each brick a tongue click
in an orchestra of construction,

each mantel a diphthong made
malleable.   Language, circular

                as a low alto vowel.

Three rings of symbols orbit
gilded lips. The sun on the second

hand eclipses the moon.
The moon cuts blue on the cusp

of a sapphire sphere.   All this

vocabulary made
circular and ornate just to say

        the same thing over and over.

Registry Room

Ellis Island, 2011

The room is unsure of how close it wants to be
to you. The ceiling's white tiles curve away,
slow and cold, while the two American flags

hang their heads down as if to catch a better glimpse.
From behind these second story rails, you watch
tourists scurry across the first floor. The cloudy day's

cream light seeps in. This is a clean room. Crisply
renovated after decades of people packed and herded
through tests and inspections. Your great-great-grandfather

hungered for something here once. Passenger
901703900105. *ALL ALIENS ARRIVING.*
You know it is hard to be an American

connecting to a place without also wanting
to own it. You want to claim this space,
to open yourself up to possession, to the passing

of ancestors anchored in your spine, let them
drift through your skin.

This does not happen.

You are still standing above a silent crowd, trying
to figure out what we owe our ghosts.

Declension

Nouns are names   are people: addition
or subtraction   of letters creates new meaning.
A closeness,   a closure, a clot.
You can now say
you've traveled   the tonal
                           shifts of the tide.

Ship   in the singular: a gift, a rift,
arisen.   How could you
expect to remain   when your name
means *foreigner*, means *train*? A bridge,
a ridge,   a receding
into waves.
             A dative relationship to the ocean
at the cost   of a genitive
                sense of home. *Dům,*
dým, dopis. Seasickness   in seven cases.
Jancovich,
Vlach, a flock of travelers. This is not
what accusative means.   New York
either ellipsis   or hyphen, determined on arrival.

Postcard I Almost Send to an Almost Lover

Krakow, 2012

I try to write about Schindler's
factory, the portraits of people
saved, the wall of faces grave

and graying, but I don't.
I know I have nothing
to say that their eyes

do not already convey.
I try to write about Poland's
dragon, the subtle slut

shame of talon and flame.
Try to be glib, to write
He only eats beautiful

virgins, so don't worry
about me! Instead, I
think of how, in Czech,

"to paint" and "to love"
are only one vowel
away: *malovat, milovat.*

The salutation alone
is written. *I paint*

you, I paint you, I paint you.

Národní Divadlo: Swan Lake

This is a love story of gold
leaf—hands that had to dance
over the ceiling's white-yellow
shine—to make a precious metal
thin enough to mold. This is
a ghost story—dancers glide
from behind burgundy curtains,
a controlled tremble on the toes.
Arms folded, then unfurled
like the wings of birds.
This is a parable—an audience
asked to sit underneath
a three-tiered chandelier
to watch women flutter their feet,
leap across stage and not be
fearful of falling. This is a family
myth—my great-great-grandfather
gilded these ceilings. This is
a metaphor—a flock of feathers,
tutus cinched at the hip. Legs
long as spondees, landings
flat as iambs: the up, the down.
This dance is a distraction—

I cannot follow the story on stage
when the rafters speak
of an ancestor—iridescent
pollen in his pores. Stardust
spackled into the cracked blisters
of his palms.

Commonly Misspelled Words

vocabulary: a splintered womb and the dream
              in which i am a wolf, stomach stone-
              laden and sinking. *this is not to drown;*
              this is to reconnect to some solid thing.

                                    :handwriting
holding my mother's face,
i smooth away the shimmer
from her lids, shadow staining
my thumbs like bruised moth wings.

semantic: what a lazy metaphor—this bridge—
              as if one thing can always reach another
              with the easy fate of a few footfalls.

                                    :accent
tonight i miss a man. once,
he pronounced *burial* like *burrow.*

once, he taught me to say *depleted* in a way
my fingers could understand. once,

comma splice: it is simple to mistake
                hibernation for a funeral.
                when this happens, say *river*
                instead of *pride*. orient grief
                as north. proceed from there.

Cartography

Morning makes itself bluer by the minute. Colder, too. In my friend's apartment, we sit in her breakfast nook while the bay window lets in light. Steam rises from broccoli omelets, the scent of garlic and salt. My friend plots today's itinerary through the tourist district, leads me to an expansive map stretched across her wall: the Czech Republic's outline etched in black. All the country's borders landlocked; the Vltava a thin, persistent reminder of thirst twisting through. She points to Malá Strana, the John Lennon Wall where people paint a layered collage of lyrics on brick. The window reminds me how cold it is outside: the snow and sudden wind. I don't know if I can give up this warmth, hands wrapped around a coffee cup. Her finger traces the itinerary, and then there it is—a small town sloping into Slovakia's northern border. *Jalubí.* A word I've never seen before but recognize the way snow knows the ground and feels it must either stick or melt, the way the bridge knows the river though they've never touched. My family has been searching for a farm in *Jalobee* for years, the town remembered as a misspelling. Here it is now, known and navigable. My friend slips small tubes of paint into her purse, asks if I'd like any particular color. "Green," I say. "Green, please."

III. Arrival

Hrad Bezděz

I.

We enter the poem   through its landscape. Our tour
           guide tries to navigate us through its lines. Mácha's
           Romantic epic "Máj"

                     now two centuries old, but we follow

its path from lake to castle and back.

The hike up the mountain's side
           is more treacherous than we've been told. Pungent
                                         pucker
of dirt we compress with each step on the trail.
           We travel along stones sculpted from the terrain's

           backbone,
a crumbled sort
           of bridge,

a safeway   among the ridges and rock-worn weariness of the
earth.

What bushes remain are burnt
           orange, careless copper flecks strewn among the soil.

Mácha opens
     his poem   with a woman waiting
on one side of the lake. She wants
     news of her lover's whereabouts. The trees scatter

their cursive
branches against the sky's ice
     blue.
               There is a thin strip
     of sky where the trees and the castle's nearest turret
          do not meet. Hrad Bezděz: its name sharp

     as spires.

II.

The terrain baits our battered tracks: soft threat
     of snap or slip with faulty step.

Past the path's stone spine, this gathering of gray on the
mountain's top.

A castle is just square structures tethered together around a turret.

Simple shapes, compact on the land,   that look
     like humble homes

if not for how history filters
everything in gold.

The tour guide tells us if we keep
       count of the stairs to the turret's top, we can
make a wish. The rhythm rocks
       a steady metronome up the steps until left, right, left

          becomes *How many left?* Three hundred, four
      hundred. I have many wishes,
but I give up
count midway.

III.

              Jarmila, the woman who waits
across the lake,   does not know her lover
                    is locked in a tower.
 I place my palm against the wall and walk
          up the stairs' slow spiral. A closer
look at my hand: one ring
      on a winter-worn finger. A silver setting
empty where once a red and heavy

          garnet was kept in place by prongs. A closer look
at the wall:

webs woven of dust—as if the stone has stolen
     skin, pulled apart the padded soft
of fingers that have forgotten

               texture's veiled teeth,
                 the rough way
             brick can bite.

IV.

             When a ship finally slides to shore,
              it is not
            who she wants.

     A messenger informs her of Vilém's
       sentence: he will die
as punishment for having killed a man who once
             seduced her. When day
                  breaks,
he will be beheaded. A turtledove twitters curses and the lake   is
the moon's
                silver mirror. Jarmila is left

with her sorrow.   I lose the guide near the top.   Stained glass
     windows are fashioned in slanted hexagonal panes,
compressed tightly like tinted coffins.
     Green, golden, clear.

It's raining now
        and I stare
at the dampened landscape.
        The twine of leafless
trees. Soil rolling and exposed, shivered into crescendos like cold
shoulders.

                                        Cast over

every pane
        of glass is a touch of mildew, a molded
tessellation dark and spreading.
Even when I climb past

                        the window, my sight still stays lined
with honeycombed edges. The rain-fresh
        grass. The black branches
and their pulse.

V.

I love a man who does not   love
        anyone except who   he thinks   he'll be one day.
        When asked why
we can't be together,
                        he says the departure is always better
        than the arrival.

VI.

Mácha's lake lays nearby. Man

        -made cavity

            constructed under the orders of Charles IV.

There is a thin tinniness to the water. Brittle. Metallic.

                    Like skin stretched too far

                        over a fresh

scar. The lake's surface ripples wildly in the seasonal spell
of winter wind.

My ring's garnet slipped out in a grocery store

        in my lover's hometown.

            Wrist deep in fresh tomatoes, my hand   emerged

soggy from the stand: fruit flesh and seeds, skin

        the stone had punctured as it loosened.

He promised to replace it. We went home and ate.

VII.

Some people think they can keep

                  count   the higher up

                         we climb.

      Each shouldering their secret

sum.

The man Vilém killed   was his own father. He had not known
this until after the body lay still.

The prison guard
is the only person
         he told his story to,   and the guard
         never   spoke   again.

              Who knows, then, how the poem came to us?

Look at the trees,
the same forest in which Vilém's band of thieves mourned their
loss.
         Notice how
shadows stain the land a cobalt shade of cold,
but the russet roofs are warmer.
              Again the dying copper bushes.

VIII.

The wind raws everything
    in its wet wake. We've made it to the turret's top, stretching
our necks over the edge.

         The hills are as far as the trees
         are tall, barren besides a few buildings, a few

cottages patched together.   Air currents stream to meet our
chapping faces.

One person leans over, opens their mouth   and
screams,
but it's rushed into silence by the gust.
                                My voice and all its pink erasures.

IX.
            At least Vilém's thieves could mourn
                        surrounded by green: warm   shades
of fir and spring's first fidgeting.
                                        Unlike Jarmila
            who could only cry
    near the lake's cold silver, the water's taunting stillness.

Someone in our group loses a black scarf—unwrapped
                from their neck by the wind. Its black fringe
                        flaps like feathers.

As the rest of the tour laughs and points,

I drop my ring over the turret's edge.
Into the current, into all the muddled

mirrors.

IV. Departure

Jalubí

A small green stone of a word. A faint
glow. I imagine it slipped
in a coat pocket, fingers frequently searching
for its smoothness as the boat coasts and cuts

across the ocean. I wonder if it sounded to them
as it sounds to me: a quick spell, a spill
of oil and water inside the lips of a bell.

If its sheen could be seen through layers
of fraying wool, a soft aquamarine.
If they said it out loud to fall asleep below deck,
to ensure a safe arrival and ward off wreckage.

I imagine they were afraid of it
being confiscated at the shores of New York
as they were herded past the man who chalked

white marks of health on the shoulders
of immigrant coats. I wonder if they knew

what to do with it next, finally standing on earth:
to plant the stone or cast it away,

> to feed it
> to the pigeons
> flocking at their feet.

Photograph: My Great-Grandfather Frank in the Fields

Jalubí, 1920s

Frank sits slouched on a stump,   faded overalls and ankles
anchored   in a pair of crop-softened   boots.
He wears a cap.   He grins.   Hoisted onto one knee,
he holds   a brown jug of homemade   liquor
   stolen from his father's secret shelf.   In the other hand,
a glass.   Though the faded image is gray and aged,

                                          green
                              pulses through. The grass
around him freshly wet, how dew draws out
the earth's organic perfume.   My mom
        says she spent her whole   childhood
scandalized by the photo.   A trick of the eye:
        the way Frank's white collar   catches
                        his raised glass, a blur that burns
away all but his middle   finger. She laughs   as she says
this, forgetting

                        most images are made from misreadings.
She says
            she never
figured out why grandma didn't take the picture down.

Portrait: Gladys Imagined as Mother

Indiana, 1950s

I always wear this dress, whether
for funerals or church. Cotton cleaned
and pressed, faded navy with buttons
lined down the chest. My daughters

scoot to the edge of the bed,
waiting to touch the tiger's eye
earrings I pair with everything.

The spill and swirl of gold in stone
rotates in their fingers. I lie, tell them
these beads are a piece of the aurora

borealis. I say this because
I always want my daughters
to look skyward.

The threads unfurl at the skirt's
end, but when one has worn
torn potato sacks, burlap bags
as coats, any smooth thing on the skin

is silk. The eldest hands back
the earrings. She swings
her knees and feet quite close
to the only thing I have

not given up for them—a can
of sweet Pepsi-Cola placed
strategically under my mattress spring.

Thoughts After the 2012 Prague Writers' Festival

How quickly I forget the words for *mother's maiden name*, translate it as *birthmark*. My grandmother was a woman with seven holes in one ear and nine in the other. I suppose that when piercing is decoration, it cannot hurt. That when distance is forewarned, it cannot blister. What translation has come to resemble: bobbing in waves, I press my fingers into peaks and watch fluid mountains eroding faster than time. I translate my grandmother into past tense, though she is still living. Two years separate us, but I aim to hang the pair of our Octobers, globed and golden, from my earlobes, casting shadows on my neck, marking flesh for ornamentation. The words I used when I asked the wind to touch me as if it couldn't recall the color blue. As if the planting of vowels into our last name made it easier to pronounce after the ocean was crossed.

Lineage

I feel most alone when I am
cold. Winter is not a blister,
a pulse and press of white
suspended in the skin. It's a fever.

I wait for it to sweat into sweeter
things: fragrance and footfalls, purple
petals puddling on the street. When

the cold loneliness settles in and steeps,
there are places that make me
feel safer. I walk through the statues
at Vyšehrad and stare at Libuše,

mythical princess who prophesized
the rise of Prague. Her gray frame
stands stark against the branches, against

the sky blanched to bone. She sweeps
her arm towards a vision that towers
only in her sight. She named it *Praha*.
She named it *Threshold*, trying to find

a word for all that can be endured.
Snow floats slowly before her stone face.
I try to hold her like a map in my mind,

even if she is looking forward
while I am reaching back.

Postcard an Almost Lover Almost Sends to Me

Raleigh, NC, 2012

You already know this winter,
this weather: January is still

more jam and back porch than cold
burn and shovel slips on ice.

You know the way honeysuckle sweats
scent; the shores of North Carolina

will still be crisp when you come back
but Europe will erode in your mind

once you leave. You can't cling to home-
sickness like snow sticking to the streets.

There is a gratitude you owe your past
and the Atlantic Ocean, both open now.

Yet you carry these gifts as grief,
memory heavy as debt.

As you learn another
language, I've been thinking

about ours. Have you ever noticed
how any one letter can start a word

but not any one pair? How the same
might be true of people?

Intonation

Save for Slovakia,   the word for *language*
changes at each   adjacent border.
A dialect,   a dilation.
A detection of proper pronunciation.
Slovo   slow-
        dripping.
                    We call this accumulation of sounds
                      vocabulary. We call it *slovník*,
shoulder it in our throats.
                      Is speech sea or shore,   safe
                      house or turbulence?
Sounds rehearsed
        and scattered on the horizon. Vertical, the verse,
                  the curse
of continuous perimeter.
                    Is there an invisible
                      threshold
                at which you must find
        a new word   for *thirst*?
        Moře nebo pobřeží,
these lines   that draw a country's   confinement?

Language freckles the landscape,   bright and bleached,

        in sun, in sonic, in eleven million speakers,

native   and   navigating.

Easter Market

Budapest, 2012

The sky is a pale green, a strange pearlescent sheen for this time of year. The spring air smells amber: warm bread and beer, sweet cream and sweat. People passing are met with packed stands on both sides of the streets, peddlers tempting their wares. For sale: egg-shaped ornaments with floral filigree carved into their wooden curves. Puffed pistachio pastries. Tiny cobalt bottles of perfume. Tea tree oil and sandalwood. Rows of amethyst and alabaster poison rings, powder hidden beneath small silver hinges. The woman behind the jewelry tries to sell me a pair of tear-drop earrings, two blue evil eyes suspended from gold posts. She tells me these will protect travelers. When did life teach her fear, to stave off the spirits on these streets? Or the woman next to us, spooning borscht into bread bowls, dressed all in maroon: her shawl, scarf, tablecloth. Maybe her late grandmother's boiled beets were once the only warmth to distract her from desolate Decembers. When did I learn to be afraid, I who give into the temptation to wear talismans from my ears? Or the man bartering bracelets of braided hemp and shells, smelling of salt and sea. Perhaps he sells them to regain control of the rolling waves—the way they lap towards him and constantly pull him back.

Women in Széchenyi Bathhouse

Budapest, 2012

Steam, like a savoir, rises over water.
Laying in the blue, older women bathe.
Heads back, necks golden and open,
flowered caps clasped over tufts of lilaced
hair. Unabashed about the fetal pleasure
of skin to water. Full-figured bodies
the poets compare to landscapes
because they cannot imagine femininity
as other than fertile. These women teach
me more about living in skin than my own
body ever has. We will all be so withered
and filled once the water has finished us.

Burning the Witches

Will the fire still whistle and spit
　　　　around my offerings? Will the flames'
　　　　strange orange syntax mourn as it melts

　　　　the flesh that once fed it? At the edge
　　　　of this Czech village, visitors are welcome
to witness the staged burning of witches.

Tonight is the stomach of spring—
　　　　midpoint between the equinox and summer
　　　　solstice. Scarecrow witches are sacrificed,

　　　　fastened with sapling to the pyre.
　　　　Since their power weakens as the weather
warms, the night will be set alight in hopes the flush

will usher them out. I stand surrounded
　　　　by a crowd of floodlit faces, sparks
　　　　sharpening the angle of every chin, every grin

　　　　cast sinister in copper shadow. And I
　　　　among them, wishing winter away
just as hurriedly but horrified

of the origins *bonfire* has in innocent bones.

        We each throw our own kind of coal

        into the young flame. Someone throws a name;

        another, an ocean. Any memory that can be used

        against us is purged. The ocean burns

green, like copper and zinc, and I want my bones

to burn, too. *V noci každá kočka černá.* Want to whisper

        that women have never been

        afraid to lean into the heat.

Jalubí

Canola fields the color of gold coins, polished by late afternoon sun. The scent of petalbreath warm in the wind—horse shit and bread. Earth unturned. The churning of butter and bitter hops. The clomping of a wagon led by two horses, a driver's wagging head and harsh whip hit. Laughter of three children hiding in the rubble of the ruined church—unwashed hair and dark-eyed stares. Spinning the Maypole's faded blue ribbons. Older woman trudging two grocery bags to her home. Such thin skin around such small bones. Lilac hair held back by silk kerchief. Knees gnarled into a vowel no language can pronounce now. A child's red bike. A tractor too rusted to be recovered. Abandoned on a dirt path. Out this far, a quiet as deep as animal tracks. A farm that may or may not have belonged to a family named Vlach—a name that could have been yours if women wore their mothers' past lives on their lips. Brick and brooms and a doorframe painted white. Windows whose broken panes whistle in the wind. A sky that may or may not be bluer than water—a color that could have belonged to you if you had worn your mother's eyes. Maybe in another life. A fence to be jumped. More fields, this yellow freshness. Fistfuls of wildflowers grown to the wrist. A remorse for not staying longer. A desire to run away with a palm full of petals. This itching suspicion that

everyone steals
but it's only the thieves
who feel guilty.

V. Arrival

I Dream of Ships Before Leaving

Ribcage ruptures formed
this earth. This water pulled
into taut hauntings, spooled
into sky once lilac-oxidized.
We, sailored. We anchored
to brick and bark; twins in
these twilights and darkenings.
Likelihood of return loosely
based on: how many of our
nine children survived; how
close the place of death was
to home. Home was once
such a bluebird refuge for us.

Thoughts on Wanderlust

History is a string of people
entering where they don't belong.

All villages settle into misspellings,
into mile markers on maps.

All heirlooms are anchors, heavy
with the pained persistence of ancestors.

Homesickness is an upset nest,
warm and empty as the sunset.

Haunt is derived from a word
meaning *to bring home.*

Somehow I feel my bones
already told me this long ago.

Mischief

Once I lost a pair of garnets,
a graduation gift. Pomegranate
seeds fashioned into earrings,
facets cut to hold light in deep

fuchsia folds. Whenever trinkets go
missing, we know to blame Gladys.
Her spirit, really, that shows itself
by hiding things. Bobby pins,

buttons, rings. Should it surprise
us, the way jewelry attracts these
hauntings? Pieces made to showcase
the body. How earrings cast shadows

on exposed shoulders, how tiny a wrist
seems when slipped into a bracelet's
obliging mouth. A necklace resting
in the slender curves of a clavicle. Isn't this

what spirits are after: a reminder
of the shapes of the bodies

they've misplaced? To enter or rest
on skin without causing harm, to stay

comfortably afloat? I dreamt,
weeks after I lost my earrings,
that they had fallen from a shelf.
And there they were in the morning,

waiting on the carpet underneath.
Bright red and ready to be worn.

Photograph: Gladys as Child

Illinois, 1920s

She's no older than thirteen,   perched
on the front stoop of her home.   Scuff-marked
Mary-Janes, a lace dress that hangs
       just above her knees.   Her hair is a tuft
of dark dandelion fluff,   unruly and spooled in thick
curls. The gene for those tresses   is expressed
every so often in the family,   which means my sister
can never smooth
her stubborn strands.   At night, I tame her tangles
with a thick comb   and patient fingers. Rough,
      rust-colored spirals I slip behind her ears.
As Gladys aged, the color faded but the wiry
curls remained. This is what heredity means:
to translate the texture
          of those who've passed
into someone breathing right beside you, to test
       if breath can bear that weight.

Photograph: My Great-Great-Grandparents

Jalubí, 1920s

Their smiles are a showcase of white,   straight teeth,
sweat tracing shadow strands   down their cheeks
until the sharp   taste of salt meets
          their tongues.   Marie's dress is coarse
fabric, white collar close to her throat.   A scarf holds
back her hair. Kleofas is in a baggy shirt,
          bunched   under faded overalls.
Two faces, two chests in front of long, leafy rows, but
          the rest   lies outside the frame.
What remains creates space for so many questions:
How much soil slides beneath
          their nails? Does a breeze
drag its cool whisper across their chapping skin?   Do
the chirps of birds blend into the field's   frenzied
cricket sounds? The only thing I can discern
          for sure through the gray picture's grain:
          the young stalks layered
          behind them are green and full, grown to
survive   season after season.

What I'll Tell My Great-Granddaughters

Not all the spells you cast will last,
especially the fearful and frantic. Never trust
tilted tulips or people who become short
of breath around shipwrecks. Anything folded
in on itself looks like a rose if held
closely enough. Wear all my jealous jewelry
on your right wrist, in your twisted hair, under
your tongue. A group of relatives you've never met
is called a garden—tend to them. Be weary
of women who stitch dried leaves
of lavender into lace window sheers—
clearly no one should believe memory
can be melted into scent. If you learn
a new language, teach it also to your shadow.
We can't have you trailing vowel sounds
behind your back in unfamiliar shades
of lilac and black. When you first visit
the city of your birth, it is best to go
with a poor sense of self—you are not the resin
that will harden into amber, not the insect
trapped inside—you are the time it took to form
the insect's wings—specifically the veining,

the green-gold sheen. And write down everything you do.
History has given up its ability to grip. The past
has a weakened grasp, and, unanchored by words,
stranger sisters have slipped through.

Time

—*after Ilya Kaminsky*

Your grandmother opens her mouth. She is telling you a story she once heard someone else tell. Instead of words, you hear the bright chirp of birds perched on her lips.

Snow: A reminder of how to hold ourselves in the cold.

Myth: Prague is a haunted garnet. You can haunt what belongs to you, but you can only steal what doesn't. I've tried to wear the city as both.

Listening: If all sounds exist at once, what does this say about our bodies?

Czech: The word tastes golden if you pronounce it slowly. You've seen your grandmother gild it.

Generation: Each winter, the water.

Reasons to Return Home

Because we disappoint the clouds by how little
our bodies change shape, so the least we can do

is move for their amusement. Because only
the splinters on your own front porch

are sharp enough to spin secrets in your skin.
Because your mother can only weather so much

worry before every morning becomes a storm
sworn to sweep out all harbors until you return.

Because postcards are just ghosts growing up
without a defined sense of home. Because

the perfumes you spilled in your suitcase
can still be worn—the scent of a wilting wreath,

waiting to be unpacked: lemon and vanilla and crabgrass.
Because a stone that rolls gathers no moss, but who

doesn't want a warm sheen of gentle green to unfold
around them, a barrier between body and unsolid ground?

Because of *migrate*'s etymology: one who trembles
when they remember they've left the tea kettle on

and must save the kitchen curtains from burning.
Because if your father has a father, then your moon

must have a moon hidden beneath the floorboards
of your childhood bedroom.

Ancestors

—after the Kiki Petrosino poem of the same title

One grieves, gorgeous as worship.
Another lies in a field the shape of your face.
One of them asks about their accordion.
There's one the color of a garnet, one like chamomile.
There's one braiding basil leaves into dough,
her aproned ghost handing out *koláče*.
You find a fir one, a fermented one. One made of honey.
One lives in cobblestones, one in the spires' sweaty reach.
One misread *Empress* as *Temptress* and has been haunting
accordingly ever since. One has finally learned to write
by watching others swim: *s* and *t*, the crests of wet shoulders.
One catches your coughs in a gold goblet.
You remember the one who begs a fevered
forgiveness for all the sickness she spread.
You've wasted so much rain waiting for
the one who refuses to appear, no matter
how sincere your summoning.
Being one person in this lineage is no more
than being one letter of a language:
written yet unaware of words.

Acknowledgements

My thanks to the editors of the following journals, in which some of these poems originally appeared, sometimes in slightly different versions and with different titles:

491: "To Karlův Most"

The Adroit Journal: "Lineage"

The Baltimore Review: "What I'll Tell My Great-Granddaughters"

Big Lucks: "Thoughts on Wanderlust"

Bodega: "I Dream of Ships Before Leaving"

The Bohemyth: "Postcard I Almost Send to an Almost Lover"

The Boiler Journal: "The Fortune Teller Predicts a Journey" and "Postcard an Almost Lover Almost Sends to Me"

Cleaver: "Cartography"

DIALOGIST: "Passport"

Green Mountains Review: "I Dream of Trains Before Leaving"

Hayden's Ferry Review: "Registry Room"

PANK: "Intonation" and "Pražský Orloj"

Plum Creek Review: "Thoughts After the 2012 Prague Writers' Festival"

The Raleigh Review: "Reasons to Return Home" and "Mischief"

Redivier: "Declension"

Rust + Moth: "Photograph: My Great-Great-Grandparents"

Sundog Lit: "Baking Lessons", "Burning the Witches", and "Reasons to Travel to Another Country"

Tinderbox: "Learning to Speak Czech: A Homophonic Translation"

Vinyl: "I Forget the Czech for 'Stamp' in the Post Office and Start Making Up Words Instead" and "Women in Széchenyi Bathhouse"

Wyvern Lit: "Commonly Misspelled Words", "Conjugation", and "Rovné a Doprava"

"Mischief" was anthologized in *Undead: A Poetry Anthology of Ghosts, Ghouls, and More* (Apex Publications, 2018) under the title "My Great-Grandmother's Ghost is a Kleptomaniac".

The first poems in this book were written in Prague in the winter of 2012 during a spell of homesickness. My thanks to the creative writing department at Oberlin College and Christopher Howell for awarding them the Emma Howell Memorial Poetry Prize.

My thanks to the University of North Carolina Wilmington and those who awarded me a Kert Green Fellowship and a Brauer Fellowship, which funded my trip to and research at The National Czech and Slovak Museum and Library. To Philip Gerard and his research class. To Sarah Messer and my peers in our book-length workshop. To Malena Mörling, who taught me to be friends with "the white ghost." To Mark Cox for his craft. To Lisa Bertini for all her hard work. To Sally J. Johnson and Katie Jones for their extended time and thoughts with this book. To EG Hendrix for calling out my "thirst"—the word only appears four times in this manuscript, which I hope is an acceptable amount. To Jake Bateman and Ashley Palmer for their friendship. To Eli Sahm.

Appreciation is extended to David Muhlena, Library Director of the National Czech and Slovak Museum and Library, Sarah Pfundstein, librarian in the Genealogy Division at Indiana State Library, and Dolores Benes Duy, Director of the Czech and Slovak American Genealogical Society of Illinois for helping to further my research.

The following books shaped this manuscript and my ways of thinking about family and language during this writing process: Christina Davis's *An Ethic*, Brandon Som's *The Tribute Horse*, Ilya Kaminsky's *Dancing in Odessa*; Patricia Hampl's *A Romantic Education*; David Bellos's *Is That a Fish in Your Ear?: Translation and the Meaning of Everything*, and Rita Dove's *Thomas and Beulah*.

Deep gratitude to the staff of CIEE Central European Studies in Prague, especially Amanda Bell for helping me navigate my homesickness and Jana Čemusová for helping me find Jalubí. To my host family Petr, Stana, Vitek, and Eliška for extending their hospitality, home, language, and culture to me. To Lucie Merhautová, whose professorship expanded my relationship with Czech literature. To everyone at Člověk v Tísni for offering me an internship. And to all the friends I made in Prague: Michala, Jakub, Tina, Emma, Kate, Max, and, of course, Ian and Eugenia—chips, dips, and hot lips.

Most importantly, I extend thanks to my family. To everyone who shared their memories of Gladys Vlach: Aunt Lynn, Aunt Jenny, Aunt Carol, Aunt Connie, and Grandma Sharron. To my siblings Ryan, Trent, and Meredith. To my parents, without whom I'd have no foundation for my adventures. And to Gladys, whose spirit told me in a dream where to find my garnet earrings. (Yes, reader, that poem is true.)

Finally, to the city of Prague itself—děkuji.

About the Author

Emily Paige Wilson is the author of *Jalubí* (Unsolicited Press, 2022) and two chapbooks: *Hypochondria, Least Powerful of the Greek Gods* (Glass Poetry Press, 2020) and *I'll Build Us a Home* (Finishing Line Press, 2018). Her work has been nominated for Best New Poets, Best of the Net, and the Pushcart Prize.

Learn more at emilypaigewilson.com.

About the Press

Unsolicited Press is rebellious much like the city it calls home: Portland, Oregon. Founded in 2012, the press supports emerging and award-winning writers by publishing a variety of literary and experimental books of poetry, creative nonfiction, fiction, and everything in between.

Learn more at unsolicitedpress.com.

Find us on twitter and Instagram: @unsolicitedp